PROPERTY OF
METHOD
FAYETTE

D1233920

WRITERS AND THEIR WORK: NO. 100

War Poets
1914-1918

By EDMUND BLUNDEN

Published for The British Council
and the National Book League
by Longmans, Green & Co.

Two shillings and sixpence net

Edmund Blunden, himself a poet of the 1914-1918 war, pays tribute in this essay to the 'soldier poets' of that conflict. He shows how Rupert Brooke's ardent response to the outbreak of war was succeeded by the savage, accurate descriptive poems of Siegfried Sassoon, and by Wilfred Owen's compassionate vision of men engaged in mutual slaughter. These are the three main figures in Professor Blunden's essay, but he reminds us of other poets: Arthur Graeme West, Charles Hamilton Sorley, Rober Graves, Julian Grenfell, Robert Nichols, F. W. Harvey, Ivor Gurney and Isaac Rosenberg. Some of these have become almost totally forgotten, since, as Professor Blunden observes, 'fame is unequal'. Yet they all played their part in upholding 'the honour and the necessity of poetry when hard times threatened to annihilate it'.

Edmund Blunden is the author of two other essays, *John Keats* and *Charles Lamb*, in the series which also includes an essay on his own work by Alec M. Hardie.

Bibliographical Series
of Supplements to 'British Book News'
on Writers and Their Work

★

GENERAL EDITOR
Geoffrey Bullough

METHODIST COLLEGE LIBRARY
Fayetteville, N. C.

45964

WAR POETS
1914-1918

by

EDMUND BLUNDEN

PUBLISHED FOR
THE BRITISH COUNCIL
AND THE NATIONAL BOOK LEAGUE
BY LONGMANS, GREEN & CO.

LONGMANS, GREEN & CO. LTD.
48 Grosvenor Street, London W.1

Associated companies, branches and
representatives throughout the world

First published 1958
Reprinted with additions to bibliography 1964
© Edmund Blunden, 1958

Printed in Great Britain by
F. Mildner & Sons, London, E.C.1

821.912
B658 w

CONTENTS

I OLDER WAR POETRY   *page* 7

II RUPERT BROOKE AND OTHERS   12

III SIEGFRIED SASSOON   22

IV MAINLY WILFRED OWEN   29

     A SELECT BIBLIOGRAPHY   39

ILLUSTRATIONS

between pages 22–23

I RUPERT BROOKE

II CHARLES SORLEY: by courtesy of K. W. Sorley, Esq., and the Cambridge University Press.

III SIEGFRIED SASSOON. Mr. Sassoon, by whose kind permission this photograph is reproduced, writes: 'it was taken by G. C. Beresford, one of the characters in Kipling's *Stalky and Co.*, and might well have been my last as the Battle of the Somme started soon afterwards.'

IV WILFRED OWEN: by courtesy of Messrs. Chatto and Windus Ltd.

¶Poems by Rupert Brooke are quoted by kind permission of Messrs. Sidgwick and Jackson; Mr. Sassoon has also allowed liberal quotation from his work; Wilfred Owen is quoted by courtesy of Messrs. Chatto and Windus Ltd.

WAR POETS: 1914—1918

I

OLDER WAR POETRY

THE poetry of war has a long past: 'fierce wars and faithful loves' have been the theme of numberless celebrated epics, lays and ballads. It is, however, largely a twentieth-century matter that this poetry has turned away from heroes and hero-worship, as indeed Milton says he did once, declining in his masterpiece

> to dissect
> With long and tedious havoc, fabled knights
> In battle feigned.

In 1816 the young poet Keats opened for the first time the translation of Homer by his Elizabethan forerunner, George Chapman, and the *Iliad* there offered him the following first lines:

> Achilles' baneful wrath resound, O Goddess that impos'd
> Infinite sorrows on the Greeks, and many brave souls loos'd
> From breasts heroique; sent them far to that invisible cave
> That no light comforts; and their limbs to dogs and vultures gave.

This approach to the subject was far from distressing Keats, as his splendid sonnet on the occasion demonstrates; in his time there was glory in it. It has happened to me, however, to hear a classical scholar of eminence speak of having grown unable to enjoy the *Iliad*; in the end Homer's repetitions of detailed slaughter exhausted him.

Since Homer in verse distributed so many 'snicks and snocks' to the combatants at Troy, war poetry has abounded; and if blind Homer himself can hardly have been an actual warrior, we observe that his successors have generally not been such. One of them, William Wordsworth, has been regarded as the highest English war poet, and in one aspect he may well hold that rank—he has in view the upholding of noble virtues. Wordsworth does not care for carnage as

7

a topic of poetry, in spite of his once asserting that carnage is an instrument of destiny. In another aspect, his war sonnets are remote from us, as when he advises his fellow-men to go into battle without apparent awareness of the realities attending on that choice.

Looking back to English poetry of the seventeenth century, we soon meet poets who were apt to grow rhetorical upon fighting by sea and by land. That 'poet of great celebrity', Edmund Waller, M.P., then wrote in an exuberance of emotion upon the leaders of the kingdom:

> Terror and death on his loud cannon waits,
> With which he pleads his brother's cause so well,
> He shakes the throne to which he does appeal.
> The sea with spoils his angry bullets strow,
> Widows and orphans making as they go:
> Before his ship fragments of vessels torn,
> Flags, arms and Belgian carcasses are borne,
> And his despairing foes, to flight inclin'd,
> Spread all their canvass to invite the wind.

That was striking war poetry in 1665. In 1666 we have John Dryden painting in language the same notion of wonderful achievements—all, again, taken from report, though infused with eagerness of imagination:

> The warlike Prince had sever'd from the rest
> Two giant ships, the pride of all the main,
> Which with his one so vigorously he press'd,
> And flew so home, they could not rise again.
>
> Already batter'd, by his lee they lay:
> In vain upon the passing winds they call;
> The passing winds thro' their torn canvass play,
> And flagging sails on heartless sailors fall.
>
> Their open'd sides receive a gloomy light,
> Dreadful as day let into shades below;
> Without, grim Death rides bare-fac'd in their sight,
> And urges ent'ring billows as they flow.

To say that in the age of Dryden poets did nothing but
extol mighty conquerors against a backcloth of wild war
effects would be wrong, but there was a long way to go
before the whole problem of settling human differences
without recourse to the argument of bloodshed was deeply
thought about. It could never be an easy question, especially
for poetic thinkers, since hatred of violence and sympathy
with suffering do not overthrow the honour of unselfishness
and valour. As the age of sensibility proceeded, the advance
of conscience to which we owe the inception of so many
reforms, the note 'I hate that drum's discordant sound'
came into our poetry. And yet it was occasional only. The
gentle recluse, William Cowper, in that gospel of sensibility
'The Task', published in 1785, started his second Book in
one direction but soon turned in another. His beginning was
a deep sigh, while he put down his newspaper and reflected:

> Oh for a lodge in some vast wilderness,
> Some boundless contiguity of shade,
> Where rumour of oppression and deceit,
> Of unsuccessful or successful war,
> Might never reach me more.

Soon, however—and who does not understand this?—
Cowper's patriotic feeling came into play, and his verse
celebrated a statesman, a general, a military success:

> Praise enough
> To fill th'ambition of a private man,
> That Chatham's language was his mother tongue,
> And Wolfe's great name compatriot with his own.
> Farewell these honours, and farewell with them
> The hope of such hereafter! They have fall'n
> Each in his field of glory; one in arms,
> And one in council—Wolfe upon the lap
> Of smiling victory that moment won,
> And Chatham heartsick of his country's shame!
> That made us many soldiers.

Yet, whether in acceptance of war as inseparable from the

scheme of things, or possibly as a form of international law and order, or in protest against its ingenious and often tremendous brutalities, few war poets in England in Cowper's days could claim any more direct experience of it than Cowper in his unsacrificed greenhouse. The same may be said of his nineteenth-century followers. They were professional authors composing at a distance from the soldier in the field. By way of example we might disinter the copious verse devoted to that astounding Sunday battle in 1815 which came to be known as Waterloo. Little or none of it came from the Duke of Wellington or any officer or man who was with him that day. (After all, they had done enough.) The poetry of that truly epoch-making battle—we are concerned with the English side—was penned by such civilians as Lord Byron, Sir Walter Scott, Robert Southey (the Poet Laureate of the time), and long afterwards by gentle Thomas Hardy. None of these great spirits had 'set a squadron in the field'.

In the early Victorian years an attempt was made by one who had certainly done his musket exercises as a volunteer to stir opinion against the god of war through a poem describing war's miseries; this ex-volunteer was Leigh Hunt, still remembered for his peace-making parable 'Abou Ben Adhem'. Not long after, Alfred Tennyson, who moved between visions of world peace and incitations to Britons to get into uniform, reported an action in the Crimea in a forceful lyric, though he personally remained in England. So the tradition ran through the nineteenth century, until George Meredith had commented on armaments and imperialism in shrewdest style, and Rudyard Kipling had spoken up for the common soldier in another manner from that of Samuel Johnson, and A. E. Housman too had sung that worthy. But so far the soldier in the emplacement or in the charge had not noticeably sung himself.

This curiosity of literary history could be examined at great length. In the end, probably the nearest that the soldier himself had come to war poetry as it was one day represented by writers of the First World War was in Elizabethan plays and poems here and there; and the thought should include Shakespeare himself, notwithstanding that his biographers have failed to discover his army identity disc. But the author of *King Henry V*, *Cymbeline*, *Coriolanus*, *Macbeth* and *Othello* knew very well what happens to men and round them in real war; he is exact in all points. The same thing can be allowed for his fellow-dramatists, for Tourneur and Webster; and in this connection, as prelude to one of the poets specially considered in our essay, Sir Philip Sidney will be named. It is still to be lamented that, as he knew war clearly, he did not live to write about it as about poetry; the more so since, in what amounted to his last action and poem, Sidney identified himself with the common soldier. That compassion or comprehension was to become the wellspring of the war-poetry of our twentieth century, when the writers were themselves for a time 'common soldiers' and in any case were constantly in touch with, and in the position of guardians of, those millions. The war of 1914 began, no doubt, with the old assumption that the poets should sit in quiet corners writing majestically about it; but that attitude did not quite satisfy readers. The title 'soldier-poets' became the brief reference to an altered view of war poetry, though what the extent of the alteration would eventually become was not at once foreseeable in 1914.

The number and the activity of the soldier-poets of Britain in the First World War were bewildering. It is still to be allowed that the man of genius is never found in large numbers. Although a multitude of interesting detached poems from all degrees and ranks of versemen belonging to the years 1914–1918 can be assembled, the dynamic poets were few, and the principal names (on the English side) are probably found in the ensuing pages. I regret the limitations of space nevertheless.

II

RUPERT BROOKE AND OTHERS

The most widely read, or quoted, of these soldier-poets of 1914–18 might be described in respect of daily concerns as nothing like the 'common soldier', as one quite worlds away in upbringing and attainment and so on—still, he was also among the millions who then left ordinary ways behind in order to serve King and Country 'for three years or the duration of the war'. Except for the great national emergency, we may now suppose that Rupert Brooke would have maintained his course as a scholar and a man of letters, and figured not as a lively sub-lieutenant but a mellowed master of a college. Peace had her victories quite enough for this competitor to win, and he was joyfully busy in winning them when the blue skies of the summer of 1914 seemed suddenly to grow mysterious with an unmeasured tempest intruding.

At that time Rupert Brooke, already a well-known personality, had reached the age of twenty-seven. As a schoolboy at Rugby, where his father was a house-master, his poetical, intellectual and athletic performances had marked him out; those who knew him (and this remained the truth in later days) were almost all taken with his gifts and his presence; his physical beauty was astonishingly in accordance with his innate imagination and enthusiasm. In due course this notable youth was elected Fellow of King's College, Cambridge, and the distinction was awarded on the merits of his dissertation 'John Webster and the Elizabethan Drama'. Years have flown, but it is permissible to fancy that had the wheel of fortune turned a little differently, the scholar-poet of King's in 1913 would be on the scene at Cambridge still. Opinions, or speculations rather, vary widely as to the predominance of the scholar, the poet, or the man of action in a grey-headed Rupert Brooke.

As things went, Brooke was a good traveller as well as a sequestered reader. In his restlessness for experiences at a distance from his own ground one might conjecture that some precognition of coming events was working. However, he was obviously born to let no grass grow under his feet; as a writer especially, this youth sped onwards. Actually he published only one volume of gathered poems, that of 1911. With it, no doubt, should be considered as part of his literary life the first volume of *Georgian Poetry*, 1911–1912. This miscellany compiled by the friend of poets (and artists) Edward Marsh gave us all a chance to read Brooke's colloquial, impulsive, day-dreaming poem 'The Old Vicarage, Grantchester', written during his wanderings out of England in 1912. In style the piece bears some likeness to Shelley's 'Boat on the Serchio' and 'Lines Written in the Euganean Hills'; in content, the emphasis is on a new generation. Persons coeval with the present writer will recollect how at that distant date before World War I some friend with an eye for the coming English poet would cordially recite such lines as:

> Here tulips bloom as they are told;
> Unkempt about those hedges blows
> An English unofficial rose.

Though Brooke the poet was not smitten with the blast of fame to which Lord Byron (one of his Grantchester ghosts) had formerly awoken, his capability of metaphysical but not exhausting verse—in 'The Fish', in 'Drawing-Room Tea'—was much admired without delay by numerous romantic readers. *Georgian Poetry* was a success, and the *Poems* of 1911 went on until, ultimately, thirty-seven impressions had been called for.

In the pre-war poems of Brooke something like a premonition can be seen recurring. A love-sonnet dated 1909 powerfully includes it:

> Oh! Death will find me, long before I tire
> Of watching you; and swing me suddenly
> Into the shade and loneliness and mire
> Of the last land!

It was there in Holbein manner in another sonnet of the following year:

> He wakes, who never thought to wake again,
> Who held the end was Death. He opens eyes
> Slowly, to one long livid oozing plain
> Closed down by the strange eyeless heavens.

In Brooke's poems of 1913 the notion of being 'beyond the sun' is one of numerous death-suggestions.

Shadows like these by no means prevented the new poet from living eagerly in the world as he walked it; they might fall upon his thought while in 1914 he portrayed 'The Great Lover', although that was a poem written largely in enjoyment concerned with the honest pleasures of the five senses. About then realism as Brooke used it was reckoned bold and decisive, and 'the rough male kiss of blankets' and 'the cold graveness of iron' were expressions sure of applause. With 'The Great Lover' we arrive at the fateful date August 1914, when the poem so named and others by the same hand came out in the third volume of the gentle periodical *New Numbers*.

The Great War made its appearance much at the same moment as *New Numbers*, Vol. III; and if 'The Great Lover' was in the nature of an adieu, it was certified such by what now happened to its author. A month after the declaration of war Brooke was given his officer's commission in that grand force, the Royal Naval Division; with very little delay he was across the English Channel and in Belgium, joining in the quick queer days when an attempt to keep the mighty German army out of Antwerp was so exciting. In December 1914, far out in peaceful Gloucestershire, the fourth and final issue of *New Numbers* was published, and it contained a group of 'War Sonnets' by

Brooke: they were not particularly remarked on at the time. Early in 1915 a new idea involved the Royal Naval Division and Rupert Brooke, who found himself on a troopship steaming towards Turkey, one of the many modern Elizabethans who were to do great things at Gallipoli and eliminate Germany's main allies from the war in a week or two. So enchantment ran.

Before he could make any noteworthy contribution to that unlucky campaign, Rupert Brooke contracted blood-poisoning. It was told me by a doctor who was at the Gallipoli landings that a scorpion's bite was the cause. The effect was that on 23 April 1915 the illustrious young poet died in a French military hospital at Scyros. He did not die without having accomplished a generous and affectionate deed for the benefit of his brother poets; for by his will he bequeathed annuities to several of them.

In *The Times* three days later Winston Churchill and another writer both drew attention to the lost poet's five 'War Sonnets' which had enriched the pages of *New Numbers*; one of them indeed had been given wider circulation when Dean Inge ('the Gloomy') quoted and eulogized it in an Easter sermon in St. Paul's Cathedral. The five were made really accessible on 16 June 1915 when they were gathered into *1914 and Other Poems* by Rupert Brooke, edited by his friend E. M., or Eddie Marsh. A few months later they were given a separate edition with the title *1914. Five Sonnets*; of this pamphlet 20,000 copies were printed. A multitude of verse books in which the war was the bardic theme, was being produced at that hour; the vision and valour of that hour had already called forth silentish Laurence Binyon's 'For the Fallen'; nevertheless the reading public mainly accepted Brooke as the poet of the war. 'This sudden fame' was not lessened when the fighting ended in 1918, as the title of a volume then added to the series of English Poets (edited by Mrs. Humphry Ward) shows exactly. 'Browning to Rupert Brooke' it was, and Brooke's share of the contents occupied seventeen pages.

Apart from the five Sonnets Brooke did not write much in allusion to the War, but the impression made by that group was such as might have been caused by some far more extensive and 'exciting' poetical performance. In what manner these Sonnets stirred the imagination and emotion of many readers in 1915 is best known through a quotation or two from Winston Churchill's prose elegy on Brooke and other contemporary notices. From 'W.S.C.': 'The thoughts to which he gave expression in the very few incomparable war sonnets which he has left behind will be shared by many thousands of young men. . . . They are a whole history and revelation of Rupert Brooke himself. Joyous, fearless, versatile, deeply instructed, with classic symmetry of mind and body, ruled by high undoubting purpose, he was all that one would wish England's noblest sons to be.' Another writer said, 'It is clear that the war surprised him and that he found in his readiness to do his duty for his country a high religious joy. These five sonnets . . . express this joy without the misgiving and emotional insecurity of his earlier verse.' To quote once more, 'The sonnets he wrote on the war are among the most beautiful of the contents of this slender volume. To him the call for sacrifice was the opportunity for purification. The feeling has never been better expressed than in the noble lines which begin the sonnet 'Peace':

> Now, God be thanked Who has matched us with His hour,
> And caught our youth, and wakened us from sleeping.

The same high spirit is everywhere manifest when he touches the great subject. The words have a joyous lilt, but the deeper music of the feeling is grave. None but a very perfect, gentle knight could have so written.' It is not intense criticism, true, but it is an honest voice from the past speaking sincerely about Brooke, as so many spoke just then.

Few of these who were in the early phase of war service as Brooke was in 1914 and 1915 and heard his 'music' will ever have forgotten it, even though they might survive

regarded as 'not so much a great poem as a great piece of
war propaganda'—just at the critical minute and as authority
and popular sentiment would have it. An excellent judge of
literature has nevertheless made the comment that this sonnet
gave us the assurance of greatness in Rupert Brooke; that is
to say, it had the power to capture instantly 'the affections
of those patriots that Kipling and Newbolt had been
wooing assiduously in a sequence of books'. The com-
mentator was the poet Sherard Vines, in the year 1927.
With his words, intended to lead the reader away to other
poems by Brooke as being superior illustrations of his
powers, one may recall the picture (in prose) of the English
volunteers of 1914, The Vision, set at the beginning of C. E.
Montague's enchanting *Disenchantment*. It was Montague's
persuasion there that 'the plain recruit who had not the gift
of a style' said to himself in his own way in the emergency
of 1914 the same thing about the immortal hour as did
Rupert Brooke the eloquent in the War Sonnets.

If a broad statement is allowable, Brooke as a war poet
belongs to the Wordsworth class. It is true that he tumbled
into war's realities briefly in the Antwerp business of 1914,
and was on the edge of the battle in 1915 when an absurdity
of fate stopped him; and yet his war poems are abstract.
The appeal that his Sonnets and those of Wordsworth in
this direction make is unconnected with the particulars of
war experience. That condition has both its advantage and
its handicap; since the actualities of battlefields and other
scenes affected by wars bring on many considerable questions
and even confuse the idyll which piped brave youth in
August 1914 onward but not always upward. That Brooke,
if he had lived to march into the horrifying battlefield of the
River Ancre with his surviving companions of the Hood
Battalion in the deep winter of 1916, would have continued
to write sonnets or other poems in the spirit of the 1914
Sonnets, is something that I cannot credit. Besides, we have
the indication that he began to turn towards the poetry of
the real War in his 'Fragment' from the troopship in April

1915, with its conversational ease but its decisive, selective speech:

> I strayed about the deck, an hour, to-night
> Under a cloudy moonless sky; and peeped
> In at the windows, watched my friends at table,
> Or playing cards, or standing in the doorway,
> Or coming out into the darkness. Still
> No one could see me.
>   I would have thought of them
> —Heedless, within a week of battle—in pity,
> Pride in their strength and in the weight and firmness
> And link'd beauty of bodies, and pity that
> This gay machine of splendour 'ld soon be broken,
> Thought little of, pash'd, scatter'd. . . .

Pity resounds, even if the meditation ends not in pity, not in hero-worship, only in an apprehension of new ghosts, the writer himself soon to be one of them. Had that apprehension been proved groundless, had Brooke been spared to pass through the Gallipoli warfare into the old Western Front and Picardy and Passchendaele, his old disposition to make his poetry lively with things as they are must surely have served him and literature memorably.

As things turned out, the opportunity of poetry went to other youths of genius, who underwent what Brooke was prepared to know at all costs in the abyss of the bloodbaths: of these some did not outlive him long. Time in such a war, however, is not measured by months. Charles Hamilton Sorley, who had endured less than six Western Front months when he was killed on 13 October 1915, had experienced that seemingly short time with profound sensibility. Few mention Sorley now, but fame is unequal. At the age of twenty he was a thinker and a writer capable of illuminating matters of permanent importance, alike in verse and in prose. When his kit was sent back to Cambridge from the trenches, a sonnet found in it summed up what was going to be uttered by fighting men of the highest poetic power in the later passages of World War I:

> When you see millions of the mouthless dead
> Across your dreams in pale battalions go,
> Say not soft things as other men have said. . . .

Extraordinary popularity befell one lyric on war from a
young officer of the best kind, named Julian Grenfell, who
died of wounds on 27 May 1915. I cannot remember that
anyone noticed other poems of his—there were some, songs
of action clanging with the vitality of a neo-Elizabethan
'compleat gentleman'. The celebrated one, 'Into Battle', has
that character too; but within its course the honour of the
cause is mysteriously involved with an inevitable, predicted
sacrifice. 'Into Battle' brings back the once familiar and, to
many, grim term 'Spring Offensive', which as will be seen
in a later page was among the inspirations of a coming poet
of the Great War. Even now Grenfell's lyric defeats
commonplace criticisms because of its inspiration; possibly
we may hear Shelley's prompting behind the words, but in
fact it was the result of *there and then* on a poetical venturer.
The words are worth close attention, though plain:

> The naked earth is warm with spring,
>   And with green grass and bursting trees
> Leans to the sun's gaze glorying,
>   And quivers in the sunny breeze;
> And life is colour and warmth and light,
>   And a striving evermore for these;
> And he is dead who will not fight;
>   And who dies fighting has increase.

If it must be so . . . . There is something else, surely. But the
time for other thoughts was not yet ripe. Grenfell's noble
poem of man and nature ended at any rate with something
like the graciousness of Rupert Brooke over the dead:

> The thundering line of battle stands,
>   And in the air death moans and sings;
> But Day shall clasp him with strong hands,
>   And Night shall fold him in soft wings.

Out of the many other soldier-poets who in their verse exhibit the transition from the much-boomed '1914 Spirit' to something like despair, and whose writings never quarrel with their individual immolations, but submit their philanthropic observations, who should be chosen where only one can find a place? The answer here, unknown as he may be today, is Arthur Graeme West. It is said that West's *Diary of a Dead Officer*, edited by the philosopher C. E. M. Joad, and gratefully read by many just not dead officers, was edited too much according to Joad's pacifism. West, an Oxford scholar, born in 1891, saw all that anybody could wish to see of the Somme battle in 1916, and was struck down by a random bullet in April 1917. To count what we lost by that rifle-shot, we have only a few printed poems at our disposal. The winner is 'The Traveller', in which West, devoted to the aesthetic Walter Pater and the old Greek god Pan, finds himself at last tramping the old La Bassée Road, which crossed the British and the German trench systems and was to be feared. A symbolic causeway, daily growing ghastlier. Here the soldier-poet lost Pater and Pan. Only remained on that desolate track Bellona, the war goddess, Macbeth's love:

> And still we fare her road alone,
>   In foul or sunny weather:
> Bare is that road of man or god
>   Which we run on together.

We have also a 'Night Patrol', dated March 1916, in blank verse. It is an early example of the expression in the manner of Henri Barbusse in France which was far from what the English soldier-poet formerly expected to produce. Of course no one will blame Rupert Brooke for unconsciously challenging the later realists to retort to his 'rich dead'. West's patrol worked over a recent battleground, and the poor dead were the principal objects they encountered:

> They lay, all clothed,
> Each in some new and piteous attitude
> That we well marked to guide us back: as he
> Outside our wire, that lay on his back and crossed
> His legs Crusader-wise: I smiled at that,
> And thought on Elia and his Temple Church.
> From him, at quarter left, lay a small corpse,
> Down in a hollow, huddled as in bed,
> That one of us put his hand on unawares.
> Next was a bunch of half a dozen men
> All blown to bits, an archipelago
> Of corrupt fragments. . . .

III

SIEGFRIED SASSOON

We come now to a very near contemporary of Rupert Brooke who in spite of his admiration of that poet came into notice largely because he interpreted war from anything but the point of view of the five Sonnets. No poet of twentieth-century England, to be sure, was originally more romantic and floral than young Siegfried Sassoon from Kent. Up to 1914 Mr. Sassoon was known, it seems, more in the hunting-field and on the cricket-ground than in the literary world. There he was a gentle amateur, who now and then published a graceful composition—but no, not wholly so. Calling himself Saul Kain, in 1913 he let loose a parody of John Masefield's 'Everlasting Mercy'—a queer active piece of work entitled 'The Daffodil Murderer'. It is in some degree a poem apart from parody, and when we reconsider what Mr. Sassoon achieved as a seer of the first Great War 'The Daffodil Murderer' is a conspicuous document. In the writer's sympathies with what wretches feel and his vigilance over the life that runs or lags every day for those, we find already the indications of his then unforeseen war poetry—an *oeuvre*.

From Mr. Sassoon's recollections of the year 1914 in prose we know in what way he took the surprise of the outbreak

I. RUPERT BROOKE

II. CHARLES SORLEY

III. SIEGFRIED SASSOON

IV. WILFRED OWEN

of World War. He may perhaps have omitted some such emotional impulses as Rupert Brooke's poems record from that mysterious time. At any rate his narration from 1914 is apt to suggest the kindly, stoical, humour-loving and observant young soldier rather than the modern Crusader (if ancient crusaders were really ferocious). In 1915 and 1916 no young soldier can have gone beyond this soldier-poet in natural enjoyment of life while he looked about him in Northern France, perhaps on some march with the whole battalion or in some outpost practice in the rear of the vast trench networks. He hardly thought more of these topics than of the fruitful countryside round the camp and its not unfamiliar agriculture.

A tumult in his own 'little world of man' nevertheless grew up, and even he, in those ever companionable and undisguised prose reminiscences of his, seems scarcely able to investigate it to the full. This tumult at last forced him to make his memorable declaration that war in its 1916–1917 phase was an atrocity, equally malicious to all warriors. It has been already intimated in this brief sketch that Rupert Brooke himself so early as the first quarter of 1915 was being borne 'darkly, fearfully afar' from the innocent (because unbombarded) self-dedications of Autumn 1914. The poems of Sorley and of Graeme West (examples merely) which have been quoted were expressions of the awareness inevitable soon after Brooke's passing, a knowledge which was for a long time kept quiet by the soldier as a soldier: 'down, thou climbing sorrow!' To make this kind of situation report to the world at large was a very difficult business, even if the individual writer could acknowledge a duty that way. Perhaps the old Western Front regarded as an expanse of destruction and deadlock was a sufficient compulsion by the time that the mines under Vimy Ridge were touched off in 1916, or when not many weeks later on a serene summer morning the battle of the Somme opened with an absurd but actual killing of myriads. And yet, even if you were a soldier-poet not blown to bits, you might not find the words for the protest against these sorrows; you might still be moved instinctively to recall the healing presences of the world you had known.

In order to illustrate my theme better, and my theme includes the distinction of Mr. Sassoon as a war poet, I take leave to draw upon personal history. Among the multitudes of us shipped to the Pas de Calais a few months before the Great Push (or Drive) of the British army in 1916, I was a verse-writer; my interests were not yet changed from what life had formed before all this chaos. Lurking in the trenches by day or prowling out of them at night, I would perforce know what a bedevilled world is, and yet to make poems about it was a puzzle. In May and June 1916, in my note-books, the grimness of war began to compete as a subject with the pastorals of peace. By the end of the year, when madness seemed totally to rule the hour, I was almost a poet of the shell-holes, of ruin and of mortification. But the stanzas then written were left in the pocket-book: what good were they, who cared, who would agree?

In a sense, as that Great War unmasked its ugliness, the problem of the legion of soldier-poets was primarily one of reporting. That denomination 'Eye-Witness', used in the first stage of the war to cover official scrapiana from the observation posts, was one which these persons ought to claim if they could not claim Coleridgean imaginations. To observe—but in the battle-smoke and battle-din that is never an easy work. Poets have observed well where it was unpleasant to stay long enough to do so. George Crabbe famously based his Tales on tireless observation, now in the workhouse, now in the saltmarsh. All are not capable of his tenacity. In 'The Daffodil Murderer' Mr. Sassoon had at least shown a liking for the truth, and that was valuable to him when, moved by deepening pain and grief and irony for the 1916 soldier in the vice of ambitious powers, he became the startling war poet of a new age. To proceed with this is to refer to his Collected Poems.

In that book we soon come upon the section of 'War

Poems: 1915–1917', which begins with the banner-bearing
poem 'Absolution'; and this may be classed as a descendant
from Rupert Brooke's little family of 1914 Sonnets:

> The anguish of the earth absolves our eyes
> Till beauty shines in all that we can see.
> War is our scourge; yet war has made us wise,
> And, fighting for our freedom, we are free.

We read on, and the poet does not delay long before
asserting that freedom has been eclipsed, and that men have
become mechanisms knowing that they are mechanisms.
By this time the diction of the war poet has changed from
that of the gonfalon and aureole world to that of the
platoon and the forlorn hope:

> Three hours ago he blundered up the trench,
> Sliding and poising, groping with his boots;
> Sometimes he tripped and lurched against the walls
> With hands that pawed the sodden bags of chalk.
> He couldn't see the man who walked in front;
> Only he heard the drum and rattle of feet
> Stepping along barred trench boards, often splashing
> Wretchedly where the sludge was ankle-deep.

No experience, I dare say, has ever been more distinctly
observed; and this is just a detail in a series of things and
thinkings which end, as dully as in those days some swift
shell would end with a sunk plop in a wet stretch of mire,
with the irrelevant death of a man who was on a working
party.

If Voltaire himself had happened to wish to destroy the
romantic predilections of Siegfried Sassoon, he would have
had considerable difficulty. 'Be near me, Beauty' might
have been this poet's motto. With what a wrench of feelings
Sassoon gave up his poetic moments not to Beauty but to
Horror may be imagined. He had been in Arcadia, and
Picardy had been very like Arcadia—it is today—but what
was it under the bombardment of two such forces as then

mutilated its uplands? Mr. Sassoon saw all. To spread the eyewitness's affidavit was far from easy. National interests were, understandably, in the way. Yet such readers as myself, however handicapped by being ourselves in the battle, were becoming acquainted with the poems by mid 1917. It was a time for serious meditation on the existing state of things. To some it appeared that in the subjugation of millions of ordinary cheerful men to the dictates of some few remote commanders the real danger of humankind was increasing. To these, while the indescribable Passchendaele of 1917 was being heaped upon them, the poetry of Siegfried Sassoon was indeed readable. It did not appear as a collection, however, till the next year; but in those days next year was looked on as being very little different—it would be the same impasse.

We have then from Siegfried Sassoon as his chief soldier-poet production what came out as a little more than a pamphlet, 'Counter-Attack'. The name-poem is one of the great achievements in it; it did not depend on the reader's having endured the agony in any particular place, but all who had known the crisis would applaud the story and the laconic commentary. Again, if 'the eye on the object' is as ample a provision for the result, poetry, as Wordsworth has told us, no soldier-poet of that period was more likely to triumph than this one. It is a peculiar question how such writers, while their own lives were in intense danger every moment, and while they attended to all their duties as young leaders of men in grotesque settings, could have the eye on the object so firmly:

> The place was rotten with dead: green clumsy legs
> High-booted, sprawled and grovelled along the saps
> And trunks, face downward, in the sucking mud
> Wallowed like trodden sandbags loosely filled;
> And naked sodden buttocks, mats of hair,
> Bulged, clotted heads slept in the plastering slime.
> And then the rain began—the jolly old rain!

In quantity, it has been said, 'Counter-Attack' was not far from the description, a pamphlet; and the objection made to it here and there was that its quality was that of pamphleteering. Such an objection was academic, for there was room for an appeal against modern war, and it was narrow, for the work was a well-varied and organized book in which observation, wit, imagination marched under the command of love of ordinary humanity. The poet's armoury was sufficient. Naturally he found use for epigrammatic pieces, and these, or some of them, have become familiar quotations:

> 'Good-morning; good-morning!' the General said
> When we met him last week on our way to the line.
> Now the soldiers he smiled at are most of 'em dead,
> And we're cursing his staff for incompetent swine.
> 'He's a cheery old card', grunted Harry to Jack
> As they slogged up to Arras with rifle and pack.
> .   .   .   .
> But he did for them both with his plan of attack.

The seven lines, in which so much conversation and experience of the long departed British Expeditionary Force are distilled, may abide with that Greek epigram translated thus:

> Tell the Spartans, passer-by,
> At their bidding here we lie.

Once on a day it was a passionate cause with many of us to urge that the war poems of Sassoon should be reverberated round the world as the angel trumpeters of Donne might have managed it; then perhaps the 'world' would have a brain-wave, give the general a long leave, rescue invaluable Harry and Jack, rescue even itself. In Cambridge, in Chelsea, probably in some of the châteaux then allotted to our General Staff, certainly in America, Sassoon's poetry found its intense admirers without delay. In retrospect, the distinction that it won was to outrun our prose on the subject of war and the ordinary man, in all detail and in significance. In Sassoon's war poems the English Muse might be held to have led all the rest, though when we turn our thoughts to the pictures of Goya or to (for instance) Daudet's tale of infantry action with the billiards-mad general in it we must moderate our encomiums.

In respect of style or method, the poems in question may have upset the feelings of many faithful followers of the English Muse. Even after Robert Browning, and after the recognition of Thomas Hardy as a poet, the conversational approach to the poetic height was often distrusted. Siegfried Sassoon chose it as one of his styles, and has done so to this day; it is a subtle art. Apparently the secret of it, and its power, comes from the combination of usual though vigorous expressions with some others that do not come up as a rule in talk. Sassoon writes, 'Do they matter? those dreams from the pit?' and the thing looks simple. His typical young officer inspects the men in the Flanders barn which for many of them is their last home on earth, and might be writing his letter to his mother about it—nearly:

> I'm looking at their blistered feet; young Jones
> Stares up at me, mud-splashed and white and jaded;
> Out of his eyes the morning light has faded.

The old Great War ended, and one trouble that followed was that Peace was not all happiness; then millions of veterans (in their twenties) began looking back to such moments as that in the barn with desire and longing. At least there had been a generosity, a unity, a trust. . . . When this mood was on, Sassoon understood it, but he saw beyond it; and in giving out his opinion of it poetically he again used the seemingly casual, cliché style, until the force of a sudden amazingly clear image arrived.

'To One Who was With Me in the War' is one example of this kind of poetry. It quietly extends into a great battle-piece, scenes and shadows of the dissolving panorama; then it turns simple, but the simplicity is piercing:

>   I'll go with you, then,
> Since you must play this game of ghosts. At listening-posts
> We'll peer across dim craters; joke with jaded men
> Whose names we've long forgotten. (Stoop low there; it's the place
> The sniper enfilades.) Round the next bay you'll meet
> A drenched platoon-commander; chilled, he drums his feet
> On squelching duck-boards; winds his wrist-watch; turns his head,
> And shows you how you looked—your ten-years-vanished face,
> Hoping the War will end next week. . . . What's that you said?

The manner needs no further commentary; and for the rest, the realism speaks for an ever remarkable truthfulness, incisive in its selected even though common language. Wordsworth had his ideas about this, we know; but he did not see them embodied in such powerful plainness.

IV

MAINLY WILFRED OWEN

It fell out that the war service of Siegfried Sassoon brought him periods of companionship with several poets who had their contributions to make to the interpretation of arms and the man, war and humanity. One was Robert Nichols, a poet chiefly lyrical; looking over past years, he depicted himself in 1914 as 'steeped in the *Chanson de Roland* and de Vigny's *Servitudes et Grandeurs Militaires*'. This visionary gleam was perhaps also controlled a little by his reading Walt Whitman. It enabled him to produce in verse, while he lay in a hospital bed, idealisms concerning such dark affrays as 'Dawn on the Somme':

> Oh, is it mist, or are these companies
> Of morning heroes who arise, arise

With thrusting arms, with limbs and hair aglow,
Towards the risen gold, upon whose brow
Burns the gold laurel of all victories,
Hero and heroes' gold, th' invincible Sun?

Thus in 1916 one poet at least, with animation, could keep
up the old strain; but Nichols knew very well, prosaically,
that dawn on the Somme just then was infinite despair. He
attempted realism about such holocausts, but oddly enough
his romantic halo lasts longer than his revolver writing.

Another of Mr. Sassoon's friends, Captain Robert Graves,
struck his path into the wilderness of war immediately after
his schooldays at Charterhouse. Born in a family of scholars,
divines, wits, poets, he had a difficult task to avoid the
muddles of the precocious. The Western Front was in a way
the very place for this young poet, with his talent for the
legend, the ballad, and mystery. *Over the Brazier* (in the
trenches braziers became very kindly) and the *Fairies and
Fusiliers* were part of the war writings of Robert Graves.
The second of these titles registers the two main directions
of his consideration as he visited his troops in the dark
trenches near Béthune; with observant senses, with curiosity
in the task of expression, Graves made many of us echo his
exact note, 'It's a queer time'. How far, as a poet, he had in
view the nature and dilemma of such all-grappling war, is
another question. His brilliant, and sometimes indignant
effusions remind me of the ancient label, 'sujets particuliers,'
now at the terrible shelled covert, now in the casualty-
clearing station. They may not amount to a 'body' of writing
but Graves wrote well.[1] Be it added that he, Nichols, and
Sassoon were all installed as poets of the war in *Georgian
Poetry* for 1916–1917, the celebrated anthology made by
Edward Marsh. It was eagerly acquired as soon as it
appeared. By the year 1917 the English reader of poetry had
no need of Tennysonian phrases about modern war.

[1] The poetry of Robert Graves, Herbert Read and the author has
already been the subject of separate consideration in this series.

Nevertheless, the principal soldier-poet who drew attention in his own way to what was happening and yet was not being duly described and evaluated was Captain Siegfried Sassoon, M.C.

The volume of *Georgian Poetry* gathered for 1917 by Rupert Brooke's friend and biographer was a contrast, as an emblem at least, to the other marks of the year 1917 in Europe. That year, in one place-name, would be called the Passchendaele year. Passchendaele is a hill-top village in Belgium, and as things stood it was the centre of a British and Belgian attack (lasting several months) on the German invaders. Nothing more tedious and bloody than the Passchendaele offensive can easily be arranged. The Somme battle had been supposed the worst, but worse could come. And English home opinion was uninformed. At this juncture, Sassoon attracted the friendship of the one poet in existence who could rival him on the argument of war. The history of his meeting Wilfred Owen in a hospital to which officers suffering from shell-shock or supposed to be so were sent is among the best-known episodes in the Lives of the British Poets of this century.

The background of that meeting, which both knew painfully well, is not so well known today. In late 1917 there was little left of the 1914 spirit. The decency between foes that had marked Christmas 1914 seemed extinct. The Great War seemed interminable. No genius of any nation looked capable of loosening the deadlock. The outpouring of young lives in frightful circumstances continued as if it would only end when all were expended. But away from the fighting, many people were 'having the time of their lives'. Under such a burden of despair Wilfred Owen, already convinced of Sassoon's mastery as a poet of truth, brought himself to knock at the door of the master's room in Craiglockhart.

The sequel was that Owen understood himself better and designed his war book (never in fact completed) with immensely greater confidence and scope than he might

otherwise have had. Today he is widely known and honoured
as a war poet, and in 1917 that would have satisfied him,
though it may be reasoned that his benevolence and love of
life would have given him his memorable place as a poet of
peace. He was unable to foresee from his war at its sullen
depths the peace which came so unexpectedly in the winter
of 1918. Owen missed the Armistice by one week. He never
dreamed that such a future was at hand. Overworked,
valiant, modest and kind, he was just a company commander
in the likeness of so many at that date; and the machine-gun
got him while he was coaxing his men over some blood-
dashed canal, in the usual way. Owen the poet had satisfied
himself during his colloquies with Siegfried Sassoon that his
compositions were not nothings, that poetry might help to
extricate humanity from this nightmare of obstinacies, and
he had elected to return to the battlefield which it was
comparatively easy for him to avoid. His new experiences
in it, apart from his obvious service as a leader of men, were
to be instituted into his projected book of verse portraying
and exposing War. This poet died at the same age—25—as
his prototype, Keats.

That fragment hastily penned by Rupert Brooke in April
1915, which has been a point in the earlier part of this
reviewal of the war poetry of those years, was never seen
or heard of by Wilfred Owen. It might have been, his
readers will remark, considering the manner but still more
the turn towards pity. The poems of Owen on war express
many aspects, as his own attempted classification shows,
but perhaps pity is the one he felt most. In 'Strange Meeting'
the ghost of the enemy soldier whom he has bayoneted,
calling him friend in the world of shades, says that he might
otherwise have made a gift to posterity. But:

> It seemed that out of the battle I escaped
> Down some profound dull tunnel, long since scooped
> Through granite which titanic wars had groined.
> Yet also there encumbered sleepers groaned,

Too fast in thought or death to be bestirred.
Then, as I probed them, one sprang up, and stared
With piteous recognition in fixed eyes,
Lifting distressful hands as if to bless.
And by his smile, I knew that sullen hall;
With a thousand fears that vision's face was grained;
Yet no blood reached there from the upper ground,
And no guns thumped, or down the flues made moan.
'Strange, friend', I said, 'Here is no cause to mourn.'
'None', said the other, 'save the undone years,
The hopelessness. Whatever hope is yours,
Was my life also; I went hunting wild
After the wildest beauty in the world,
Which lies not calm in eyes, or braided hair,
But mocks the steady running of the hour,
And if it grieves, grieves richlier than here.
For by my glee might many men have laughed,
And of my weeping something had been left,
Which must die now. I mean the truth untold,
The pity of war, the pity war distilled . . .'

The conclusion of 'Insensibility' is a solemn condemnation of those with no compassion for the victims of the fighting:

By choice they made themselves immune
To pity and whatever grieves in man
Before the last sea and the hapless stars;
Whatever mourns when many leave these shores;
Whatever shares
The eternal reciprocity of tears.

Again, preparing a preface for the book that he designed, Owen insisted, 'Above all, this is not concerned with Poetry. The subject of it is War, and the pity of War. The Poetry is in the pity.' Be it noted that Owen had no tolerance for amateurish elegies such as the time teemed with—calling them 'poets' tearful fooling'. Finally a true word on Owen's quality of pity is found in his friend's introduction to the selection of poems published in 1920. 'He never wrote his poems (as so many war poets did) to make the effect of a personal gesture. He pitied others; he did not pity himself.'

The book of verse which Owen designed and in a few months would have perfected was of similar extensive view to Siegfried Sassoon's *Counter-Attack*. He was brandishing a lance like Shakespeare in the eyes of ignorance, and the flashing light was many-coloured. The scribbled sheet of paper outlining war's traits as he classified them manifests his commanding mind and would do so even if he had been unable to make poetry of them. In 1914, when he was aged only twenty-one, his immature verse at any rate spoke for his breadth of vision and his ability to sum things up. After 1914 when as poet he had shed a certain weak luxuriousness through his ordeal by battle, with intervals for reflection and analysis, his intellectual advance was swift. In many respects Owen was what is called a typical young officer, well in control of his duties, meeting emergencies with good sense, at the same time ready with the usual dry comments on the daily round and idle authority. But very few young officers had also his profound interest in the great subjects of the world's destiny. We meet with a spiritual and mental dignity, with a solitariness of imaginative purpose, in many of his poems; by that quality, it may be, his individual genius is most clearly distinguished.

'The Show' is one of the poems referred to, with its opening line 'My soul looked down from a vague height with Death' and its unveiling of a stupendous, automatic, painful scene of modern war—almost the hieroglyph of the end or the denial of our civilization. This is of the order of those panoramas in Thomas Hardy's *Dynasts*, or of the Vision of Dante. The poet's high imagination is voiced with a clear certainty. Such compositions might justify wonder even in a critic when it is remembered what the author's situation was, either involved in the mud-pits and barrages he describes or about to be among them. Imagination triumphs.

But it is not only in such allegorical pieces that Owen the poet is seen above the battle in which as a soldier he was

desperately engaged. A number of original and under-
standing essays or odes on human nature—for instance,
'Insensibility', 'Greater Love' or the more pictorial 'Spring
Offensive'—were written with singular devotion. Wisdom
and art in them were united while the poet as his first
editor remarks quite forgot his own case. This richness of
thought and word reminds us always that Keats was his
idol, and if Keats could know that he had a worshipper so
congenial and so equally capable of taking his themes far
beyond his own actual afflictions he would be happy. In
Keats's lines on negative capability in 'Hyperion' something
very like the selfless power of Owen's war poems is defined:

> to bear all naked truths,
> And to envisage circumstance, all calm,
> That is the top of sovereignty.

It is true, of course, that some of the poems are not calm,
but imprecatory and scalding; it could not have been otherwise, the urgency being that of a cry from the depths, as
one devastating day or night seized the humble heroes or
conscripts.

Nothing has yet been said here of the radiant art of poetry
which Owen practised, and which was progressive. It is
not out of place to glance at it, for deeply considered
technique itself was part of the offering that this soldier-poet
made to eventual peace and mercy. He was what
Wordsworth called Coleridge, 'an epicure in sound', he
gathered a copious and various vocabulary partly because
of the musical values of words. With Keats he delights in
slow movements, full tides of stresses. He plays with
alliteration finely, and with internal rhyme. Owen's
assonances in place of rhymes have made him a name
among later poets and prosodists. Verlaine, whose poems
like many others by French writers were part of his inner
life, may have helped him to think over this novelty of
assonances, which in 'Strange Meeting' especially is so
integral. The bitterness of his heart required some discord in

the utterance. Lastly, what an excellent writer of sonnets he became! To concentrate meaning and metaphor within that enduring form was no doubt a pleasure to him, a trial of art, even if the topic was pain and grief.

ANTHEM FOR DOOMED YOUTH

What passing-bells for these who die as cattle?
Only the monstrous anger of the guns.
Only the stuttering rifles' rapid rattle
Can patter out their hasty orisons.
No mockeries for them; no prayers nor bells,
Nor any voice of mourning save the choirs—
The shrill, demented choirs of wailing shells;
And bugles calling for them from sad shires.

What candles may be held to speed them all?
 Not in the hands of boys, but in their eyes
Shall shine the holy glimmers of goodbyes.
 The pallor of girls' brows shall be their pall;
Their flowers the tenderness of patient minds,
And each slow dusk a drawing-down of blinds.

As I take leave of Owen and the poets who may most justly be grouped with him, for the present, it is with regret that no more of that beloved generation can be discussed now. Those who are outside the scope of my essay may not have been quite of the general importance of Brooke, Sassoon and Owen in particular; but many often wrote 'something different' and something welcome to the soldier-reader. The Gloucestershire pair, F. W. Harvey and Ivor Gurney, will be friends of the survivors of 1914–1918 until the volume slips from the cold hand: many still bless the remembrance and feel the passionate idea of Isaac Rosenberg. It is much lamented that his actual war poems are not more numerous; and he is not the only instance of this. Yet these names only appear as reminders of the many who, on the English side, upheld the honour and the necessity of poetry where hard times threatened to annihilate it and its inheritors.

Probably the fiftieth anniversary of the strange outburst of the 'Kaiser-War' will be the occasion of various retrospects of the 'Soldier-Poets' (it was almost a technical term) who for some reason flourished awhile in England. I have a poor memory, but I believe one of them had the name and rank Captain William Shakespeare.

WAR POETS 1914–1918

A Select Bibliography

(Place of publication London, unless stated otherwise)

Note: The following check-list contains the works in verse of the writers discussed, arranged according to their place in the text. Prose works, letters, etc., are listed where relevant. Select bibliographies of Herbert Read, Robert Graves and Edmund Blunden are appended to the essays on these writers in the present series. Their Collected Poems covering the war period are listed below in the final section.

I. GEORGIAN POETRY, ed. E. Marsh (1911–12, 1913–15, 1916–17, 1918–19, 1920–22).

UP THE LINE TO DEATH: THE WAR POETS 1914–18, ed. B. Gardner (1964) —with a Foreword by E. Blunden.

ENGLISH POETRY OF THE FIRST WORLD WAR, by J. R. Johnston (1964) —a detailed study of the leading poets of the war.

II. RUPERT BROOKE

Bibliography:

A BIBLIOGRAPHY, by G. Keynes (1954).

Collected Works:

COLLECTED POEMS: WITH A MEMOIR BY E[dward]. M[arsh]. (1918).

THE POETICAL WORKS, ed. G. Keynes (1946).

THE PROSE, ed. C. Hassall (1956).

Separate Works:

POEMS (1911).

1914 AND OTHER POEMS (1915).

JOHN WEBSTER AND THE ELIZABETHAN DRAMA (1916).

LETTERS FROM AMERICA, with a Preface by H. James (1916).

Critical Studies:

RUPERT BROOKE AND THE INTELLECTUAL IMAGINATION, by W. de la Mare (1919).

RECOLLECTIONS OF RUPERT BROOKE, by M. Browne (1927).

RED WINE OF YOUTH: A LIFE OF R. BROOKE, by A. J. A. Stringer. Indianapolis (1948).

RUPERT BROOKE, by C. Hassall (1964).

II. CHARLES SORLEY

> MARLBOROUGH AND OTHER POEMS. Cambridge (1916).
>
> LETTERS FROM GERMANY. Cambridge (1916).
>
> THE LETTERS, WITH A CHAPTER OF BIOGRAPHY. Cambridge (1919).

II. JULIAN GRENFELL

> BATTLE. Flanders (1915).
>
> JULIAN GRENFELL, by V. Meynell (1917)
>
> —a memoir, with poems.

II. LAURENCE BINYON

Collected Works:

> THE FOUR YEARS: WAR POEMS (1919).
>
> COLLECTED POEMS, 2 vols. (1931).

Separate Works:

> THE ANVIL (1916).
>
> THE CAUSE: POEMS OF THE WAR (1917).
>
> FOR THE FALLEN (1917).

III. SIEGFRIED SASSOON

Collected Works:

> THE WAR POEMS (1919).
>
> THE COMPLETE MEMOIRS OF GEORGE SHERSTON (1937). *Prose*
>
> —includes *Memoirs of a Fox-Hunting Man; Memoirs of an Infantry Officer;* and *Sherston's Progress.*
>
> COLLECTED POEMS (1947).

Separate Works:

> THE OLD HUNTSMAN AND OTHER POEMS (1917). *Verse*
>
> COUNTER-ATTACK AND OTHER POEMS (1918). *Verse*
>
> PICTURE SHOW. Cambridge (1919). *Verse*
>
> SATIRICAL POEMS (1926). *Verse*
>
> —with additional poems, 1933.
>
> THE HEART'S JOURNEY (1927). *Verse*
>
> MEMOIRS OF A FOX-HUNTING MAN (1928). *Memoirs*
>
> MEMOIRS OF AN INFANTRY OFFICER (1931). *Memoirs*
>
> SHERSTON'S PROGRESS (1936). *Memoirs*
>
> SHERSTON'S JOURNEY, 1916–1920 (1945). *Memoirs*

III. A. G. W[EST].

> THE DIARY OF A DEAD OFFICER: BEING THE POSTHUMOUS PAPERS (1918).

IV. WILFRED OWEN

Collected Works:

> POEMS, with an Introduction by S. Sassoon (1920).
>
> THE POEMS, ed. E. Blunden (1931)
> —includes new poems, and a notice of his life and work.
>
> COLLECTED POEMS, ed. C. Day Lewis (1963)
> —the definitive edition. Contains a long Introduction by Day Lewis, and a reprint of Blunden's Memoir from the 1931 edition.

Critical Studies:

> WILFRED OWEN: A CRITICAL STUDY, by D. S. R. Welland (1950)
>
> JOURNEY FROM OBSCURITY: WILFRED OWEN 1893–1918, by H. Owen (1963–)
> —the first volume of this projected trilogy by the poet's younger brother was published in 1963, and the second in 1964. The final volume is due to appear in 1965, and a collection of the poet's letters is being prepared by H. Owen and J. Bell.

IV. ISAAC ROSENBERG

Collected Works:

> POEMS, ed. G. Bottomley (1922)
> —with a Memoir by L. Binyon.
>
> COLLECTED WORKS, ed. G. Bottomley and D. Harding (1937)
> —poems, prose, letters and drawings.
>
> COLLECTED POEMS, ed. G. Bottomley and D. Harding (1949).

Separate Works:

> NIGHT AND DAY (1912).
>
> YOUTH (1915).

IV IVOR GURNEY.

> SEVERN AND SOMME (1917).
>
> WAR'S EMBERS, AND OTHER VERSES (1919).
>
> POEMS, with a Memoir by E. Blunden (1954).

IV. F. W. HARVEY

A GLOUCESTERSHIRE LAD AT HOME AND ABROAD (1916).

GLOUCESTERSHIRE FRIENDS: POEMS FROM A GERMAN PRISON CAMP (1917).

DUCKS AND OTHER VERSES (1919).

COMRADES IN CAPTIVITY: A RECORD OF LIFE IN SEVEN GERMAN PRISON CAMPS (1920).

FAREWELL (1921).

SEPTEMBER AND OTHER POEMS (1925).

GLOUCESTER: A SELECTION FROM THE POEMS. Edinburgh (1947).

IV. ROBERT NICHOLS

INVOCATION: WAR POEMS AND OTHERS (1915).

ARDOUR AND ENDURANCES (1917).

SUCH WAS MY SINGING: A SELECTION FROM POEMS 1915–1940 (1942).

AN ANTHOLOGY OF WAR POETRY, ed. R. Nichols (1943)
—contains a long Preface by Nichols.

Supplementary Selection: alphabetically, under Authors.

POEMS, 1914–1930 by Edmund Blunden (1930).

UNDERTONES OF WAR, by Edmund Blunden (1928). *Prose*
—the World's Classics edition, 1956, has a new Preface.

THE COLLECTED POEMS, by James Elroy Flecker (1916).

COLLECTED POEMS, 1905–1925, by Wilfred Gibson (1926).

COLLECTED POEMS, 1914–1947, by Robert Graves (1948).

THE COMMON ASPHODEL, by Robert Graves (1949). *Criticism*
—contains observations on poets of World War I.

IN PARENTHESIS, by David Jones (1937). *Verse and Prose*

THE COLLECTED POEMS OF HAROLD MONRO, ed. A. Monro (1933).

COLLECTED POEMS, 1913–1925 by Herbert Read (1926)
—amplified in later editions.

COLLECTED POEMS, by Edward Thomas (1920).

An important collection of volumes of War Poetry (1914-18) belongs to the Birmingham Public Libraries: Reference Department. It was presented in memory of Private W. J. Billington, and contains the poetry of many nations. A catalogue was issued in 1921 by the Department but is now out of print.

METHODIST COLLEGE LIBRARY
Fayetteville, N. C.   45964

WRITERS AND THEIR WORK

General Editor: GEOFFREY BULLOUGH

The first 55 issues in the Series appeared under the General Editorship of T. O. BEACHCROFT
Issues 56-169 appeared under the General Editorship of BONAMY DOBRÉE

General Surveys:

THE DETECTIVE STORY IN BRITAIN: Julian Symons

THE ENGLISH BIBLE: Donald Coggan

ENGLISH HYMNS: Arthur Pollard

ENGLISH MARITIME WRITING: Hakluyt to Cook: Oliver Warner

THE ENGLISH SHORT STORY I: & II: T. O. Beachcroft

ENGLISH SERMONS: Arthur Pollard

ENGLISH TRAVELLERS IN THE NEAR EAST: Robin Fedden

THREE WOMEN DIARISTS: M. Willy

Sixteenth Century and Earlier:

FRANCIS BACON: J. Max Patrick

CHAUCER: Nevill Coghill

LANGLAND: Nevill Coghill

MALORY: M. C. Bradbrook

MARLOWE: Philip Henderson

SIDNEY: Kenneth Muir

SKELTON: Peter Green

SPENSER: Rosemary Freeman

WYATT: Sergio Baldi

Seventeenth Century:

SIR THOMAS BROWNE: Peter Green

BUNYAN: Henri Talon

CAVALIER POETS: Robin Skelton

CONGREVE: Bonamy Dobrée

DONNE: F. Kermode

DRYDEN: Bonamy Dobrée

ENGLISH DIARISTS: Evelyn and Pepys: M. Willy

JOHN FORD: Clifford Leech

GEORGE HERBERT: T. S. Eliot

HERRICK: John Press

HOBBES: T. E. Jessop

BEN JONSON: J. B. Bamborough

LOCKE: Maurice Cranston

ANDREW MARVELL: John Press

MILTON: E. M. W. Tillyard

SHAKESPEARE: C. J. Sisson

SHAKESPEARE:

CHRONICLES: Clifford Leech

EARLY COMEDIES: Derek Traversi

FINAL PLAYS: F. Kermode

GREAT TRAGEDIES: Kenneth Muir

HISTORIES: L. C. Knights

LATER COMEDIES: G. K. Hunter

POEMS: F. T. Prince

PROBLEM PLAYS: Peter Ure

ROMAN PLAYS: T. J. B. Spencer

THREE METAPHYSICAL POETS: Margaret Willy

IZAAK WALTON: Margaret Bottrall

Eighteenth Century:

BERKELEY: T. E. Jessop

BLAKE: Kathleen Raine

BOSWELL: P. A. W. Collins

BURKE: T. E. Utley

BURNS: David Daiches

WILLIAM COLLINS: Oswald Doughty

COWPER: N. Nicholson

CRABBE: R. L. Brett

DEFOE: J. R. Sutherland

FIELDING: John Butt

GAY: Oliver Warner

GIBBON: C. V. Wedgwood

GOLDSMITH: A. Norman Jeffares

GRAY: R. W. Ketton-Cremer

JOHNSON: S. C. Roberts

POPE: Ian Jack

RICHARDSON: R. F. Brissenden

SHERIDAN: W. A. Darlington

CHRISTOPHER SMART: G. Grigson

SMOLLETT: Laurence Brander

STEELE AND ADDISON: A. R. Humphreys

STERNE: D. W. Jefferson

SWIFT: J. Middleton Murry

HORACE WALPOLE: Hugh Honour

Nineteenth Century:

MATTHEW ARNOLD: Kenneth Allott

JANE AUSTEN: S. Townsend Warner

BAGEHOT: N. St. John-Stevas

THE BRONTË SISTERS: P. Bentley

BROWNING: John Bryson

SAMUEL BUTLER: G. D. H. Cole

BYRON: Herbert Read

CARLYLE: David Gascoyne

LEWIS CARROLL: Derek Hudson

CLOUGH: I. Armstrong

COLERIDGE: Kathleen Raine

DE QUINCEY: Hugh Sykes Davies
DICKENS: K. J. Fielding
DISRAELI: Paul Bloomfield
GEORGE ELIOT: Lettice Cooper
FITZGERALD: Joanna Richardson
MRS. GASKELL: Miriam Allott
GISSING: A. C. Ward
THOMAS HARDY: R. A. Scott-James
HAZLITT: J. B. Priestley
HOOD: Laurence Brander
G. M. HOPKINS: Geoffrey Grigson
T. H. HUXLEY: William Irvine
KEATS: Edmund Blunden
LAMB: Edmund Blunden
LANDOR: G. Rostrevor Hamilton
MACAULAY: G. R. Potter
MEREDITH: Phyllis Bartlett
JOHN STUART MILL: M. Cranston
WILLIAM MORRIS: P. Henderson
NEWMAN: J. M. Cameron
PATER: Iain Fletcher
PEACOCK: J. I. M. Stewart
ROSSETTI: Oswald Doughty
RUSKIN: Peter Quennell
SIR WALTER SCOTT: Ian Jack
SHELLEY: Stephen Spender
R. L. STEVENSON: G. B. Stern
SWINBURNE: H. J. C. Grierson
TENNYSON: F. L. Lucas
THACKERAY: Laurence Brander
FRANCIS THOMPSON: P. Butter
TROLLOPE: Hugh Sykes Davies
OSCAR WILDE: James Laver
WORDSWORTH: Helen Darbishire

Twentieth Century:

W. H. AUDEN: Richard Hoggart
HILAIRE BELLOC: Renée Haynes
ARNOLD BENNETT: F. Swinnerton
EDMUND BLUNDEN: Alec M. Hardie
ELIZABETH BOWEN: Jocelyn Brooke
ROBERT BRIDGES: J. Sparrow
ROY CAMPBELL: David Wright
JOYCE CARY: Walter Allen
G. K. CHESTERTON: C. Hollis
WINSTON CHURCHILL: John Connell
R.G. COLLINGWOOD: E.W.F. Tomlin
I. COMPTON-BURNETT:
            Pamela Hansford Johnson
JOSEPH CONRAD: Oliver Warner

WALTER DE LA MARE: K. Hopkins
NORMAN DOUGLAS: Ian Greenlees
T. S. ELIOT: M. C. Bradbrook
FIRBANK & BETJEMAN: J. Brooke
FORD MADOX FORD: Kenneth You
E. M. FORSTER: Rex Warner
CHRISTOPHER FRY: Derek Stanfor
JOHN GALSWORTHY: R. H. Mottr.
ROBERT GRAVES: M. Seymour-Sm
GRAHAM GREENE: Francis Wyndh.
L. P. HARTLEY & ANTHONY POWEI
            P. Bloomfield and B. Bergo
A. E. HOUSMAN: Ian Scott-Kilvert
ALDOUS HUXLEY: Jocelyn Brooke
HENRY JAMES: Michael Swan
JAMES JOYCE: J. I. M. Stewart
RUDYARD KIPLING: B. Dobrée
D. H. LAWRENCE: Kenneth Young
C. DAY LEWIS: Clifford Dyment
WYNDHAM LEWIS: E. W. F. Toml
KATHERINE MANSFIELD: Ian Gord
JOHN MASEFIELD: L. A. G. Strong
SOMERSET MAUGHAM: J. Brophy
EDWIN MUIR: J. C. Hall
J. MIDDLETON MURRY: Philip Mai
GEORGE ORWELL: Tom Hopkinson
POETS OF THE 1939-45 WAR:
                        R. N. Curr
POWYS BROTHERS: R. C. Church
J. B. PRIESTLEY: Ivor Brown
HERBERT READ: Francis Berry
BERTRAND RUSSELL: Alan Dorwar
BERNARD SHAW: A. C. Ward
EDITH SITWELL: John Lehmann
OSBERT SITWELL: Roger Fulford
C. P. SNOW: William Cooper
STRACHEY: R. A. Scott-James
SYNGE & LADY GREGORY:
                        E. Coxhea
DYLAN THOMAS: G. S. Fraser
EDWARD THOMAS: Vernon Scannel
G. M. TREVELYAN: J. H. Plumb
WAR POETS: 1914-18: E. Blunden
EVELYN WAUGH: Christopher Holl
H. G. WELLS: Montgomery Belgion
CHARLES WILLIAMS: J. Heath-Stubl
VIRGINIA WOOLF: Bernard Blacksto
W. B. YEATS: G. S. Fraser
ANDREW YOUNG & R. S. THOMAS
            L. Clark and R. G. Thom